The Energy Arts

By

Charlie Fox

www.theenergyarts.co.uk

ISBN 978-0-9564997-7-6

Published by Charlie Fox
Visit my website at:
www.theenergyarts.co.uk
First Printing: August 2014

"If you want to find the secrets of the universe, think in terms of energy, frequency, and vibration..."

- Nikola Tesla

"And he is before all things, and by him all things consist."

- Colossians 1:17

King James Bible

"Do or Do not, there is no try."

- Minch Yoda

Acknowledgements

To the Creator, without whom nothing would exist to write about,

Everyone I have met and have yet to meet who further teaches me about the different aspects of personality and energy I haven't known yet, my son, who continues to inspire me to greater heights, my parents, for their endurance and fortitude which have made me a better warrior in my heart. To you all who read this, that I may have helped you to further your own journeys, and encouraged you to forge your own path upon the way.

About the Author

Charlie Fox is 41 years old and has just started The Energy Arts school in Sheffield, UK. This book is the basis of his teaching.

He is available for workshops, seminars, and appearances worldwide, subject to conditions.

Further online Lessons with email support are available through

www.theenergyarts.co.uk

The body is all about the mind.

The mind is all about energy.

Foreword

As this book is also a lesson, I have taken the liberty of repeating and reiterating certain fundamental points to make a good grounding for your practice to develop. And have split it into usable courses and lessons.

However, do remember, that a book cannot be a substitute for a good teacher, just as knowledge is not the same as wisdom. Conversely also remember, this is YOUR journey, and no-one else is responsible for it.

Safety Note:

It is advisable to check with your doctor before embarking on any exercise programme. The Energy Arts should not be considered a replacement for medical treatment; a physician should be consulted in all matters relating to health and particularly in respect of pregnancy and symptoms which may require diagnosis or medical attention. While the advice and information in this book is believed to be accurate, neither the author nor the publisher can accept any legal responsibility for any injury or illness sustained while following the suggestions made herein.

Contents

Introduction To Meditation and The Energy Arts

In the energy arts teachings ritual and ego is the enemy.

Many systems teach with rituals and over-elaborated techniques for no other reasons than shrouding it in mystery, creating a hierarchy of knowledge or making more money out of teaching it.

The effect of this has been that meditation and energy, rather than being viewed as a normal part of living has become an evil entity in many people's minds.

That is through ignorance. It is also that an empowering technique in this world is kept for the elite, where as it should be open to anyone. Keeping it 'evil' is a good way to keep people from discovering it.

To suggest that learning to control our own bioenergy and sympathetic functions is caused by evil spirits or is evil is ridiculous. As human beings we run on electricity. It is mindal, only touching upon the world of the spirit by virtue of moral behavior and values.

Many world systems from which these systems have originated have stopped short of acknowledging a God or have made brief passing references to avoid religiosity or to go along with cultural tradition. However Taoism refers directly to 'the source' of energy without naming or personalizing it, and the Zen tradition consistently refers to 'heaven' and the spiritual world in words of their own experience not with evil or sacrilegious intent.

In dealing with what presently to science is something of an unquantified and 'phantom' concept, I'd say to those who find it hard to believe in the invisible to suspend learned facts in favour of experienced truth, you'll get there more quickly.

I can teach you everything you need to know about energy in a five minute conversation, but you won't be able to do anything with that knowledge, so some techniques ARE necessary.

I include examples from different world systems which make for a good start in fundamental use of meditation and energy. From this you must find your own way, it will be a unique journey for you, even as it is common. It is simple, yet complicated.

The first course is meditation only, though it will touch on energy use in places as they are intertwined.

The second course is energy, and will also touch on meditation.

The third and final course deals with the actual applications of energy and meditation TOGETHER in contexts such as, but not limited to, the martial arts. Again this is a good vehicle for illustration.

The energy arts cannot increase your spirituality, it is **NOT** mind body and spirit, you can only achieve spirit through love and understanding of others, it is not a self - focused process. You can advance your spirituality by helping someone in need, not by focusing your own mind.

It takes **TIME**. It won't take five minutes. You are learning to use parts of yourself you haven't used before consciously, it's like learning to walk again. Be patient, also before learning how to use energy, you must become AWARE of it.

I am not a beautiful woman with an amazing figure. Following an image won't get you where you want to go.

I don't even pretend to look like a male dancer or Hollywood icon or anything remotely clean cut. On the videos and the photos I dress in normal street clothes and I am relatively scruffy.

Energy and meditation is not a sales pitch, this styling is deliberate and meant to make you look at and appreciate the content of the course and not me. The less you concentrate on what you can see and instead feel what you can feel and experience, you will get much more out of this course.

13

It is not meant to be a complete theoretical knowledge, I pick and choose whatever concepts and definitions match my own experience for illustration, these courses are practical in nature and tell you what you need to know for your knowledge to be functional.

To what degree it is functional depends on your degree of commitment and application to the journey.

These courses will use common already existing exercises with a twist and original ones I have especially created for this publication.

For ease let us explore a definition of the word 'Meditation':

Derived from the Latin meditation, from the verb meditari, ("to think, contemplate, devise, ponder"),the English term "meditation" has been introduced as a reference for Eastern spiritual practices, commonly referred to as Dhyāna in Buddhism and Hinduism, coming from the Sanskrit root dhyai, - to contemplate or meditate.

The term **"meditation"** in English can also refer to practices in Islamic Sufism, or other emerged traditions such as Christian Hesychasm, the Quaker church or Jewish Kaballah. Historical devotees have noted that "the term 'meditation' as it is used contemporarily runs concurrently to the term "contemplation" in Christianity, though typically, practices similar to modern forms of meditation were simply called 'prayer'. The Devotional, scriptural or thematic forms of meditation typically stemming from Christian, Judaic and Islamic tradition, while traditional forms of meditation derived from Asia are more often than not seen as purely technical in their implementation.

hāgâ (Hebrew: הגה) , In the Old Testament, means to sigh or murmur, or meditate.

When the Hebrew Bible was translated into the Greek:

- *hāgâ - melete*

Then into the Latin:

- *melete into meditatio*

The 12th-century monk Guigo II using the term to refer to a formal step by step process of meditational practice.

In Tibet, 'Gom' is translated as 'to become familiar with oneself' and implies a strong motivation to develop a powerful, positively moral and compassionate state of mind.

If an encapsulate book were to be written on the subject of meditation, it would be huge and every school of thought on the planet, every expression of faith or culture would have an input. The fact is, the moment man began to think, he began to meditate, to focus upon his problems and joys and sorrows.

From this we can see that the practice of meditation is and has always been universal, and anything universal has common functional aspects. This is what has been distilled into the Energy arts course.

All these exercises should be done for as long as comfortable effort can be maintained.

The Energy Arts Course 1: Meditation

Meditation

Course 1 - Beginner

Principles to consider:

- Posture/breath/focus

Exercise 1: Being aware of breath / focusing on breath and floating mind on top - learning to ignore the chatter

Exercise 2: Reflection - Don't forget to write down your own thoughts and experiences on these exercises for assessment.

Any position can be used for meditation, as long as it's comfortable so as not to be distracting, promotes proper breathing and good posture. This is a classic meditation posture.

Even lying prostrate can be a good meditation posture, it is one of the hardest to use however as this posture also promotes the sleep response! So the mind must be very focused to avoid nodding off.

Meditation is foremost about the mind, not the body, so it is good to isolate the mind by having the body in a familiar easily supportable position which the body can maintain for minutes at a time.

A good posture is important for maintaining oxygenation and energy flow.

Clothing should be comfortable and loose fitting, environment (at first) should be quiet and also comfortable in temperature. Though we should be able eventually to meditate amidst chaos, it's good to create optimal conditions when we first start to learn.

We should be trying to develop reverse breathing throughout these first exercises, as we breathe as a baby, as we breathe in the belly goes out, as we breathe out the belly goes in.

The First Key Is Breath

First and foremost, we begin meditation with a key to bring our mind back to when it strays. The first key is breath. When we consciously control our breath and focus our mind upon it. This most simple function of our lives (breathing) provides us with an **ON BOARD METRONOME** which we can both control and leave on auto pilot.

Breathing is a focus for meditation.

This first exercise using breath for focus is very simple but it's the foundation for your journey into learning more about your own self and how to control yourself to a greater extent.

In this first exercise you will begin to learn how to focus past the chatter of the mind, the anxieties and perpetuating thoughts which are an integral part of our conscious daily thought, but can also leave us feeling anxious, tense, and with a dissipated energy.

Exercise: 'Silencing The Monkey'

Find a comfortable posture, as discussed previously, and relax into it.

Close your eyes and become very aware of your breath. Make it a conscious action so you focus on it, breathe deeply and slowly, in through your nose and out through your mouth. This is a cleansing kind of breath.

As you keep trying to focus on your breath, you will find that your mind will throw up all sorts of thoughts which threaten to distract you, this is 'the monkey' chattering away. You may get distracted and your mind goes off on a tangent following these thoughts, when you realize you have strayed, don't be annoyed or frustrated, just bring your attention back to your breath and start again. This exercise is a process and it will take considerable practice to reduce the 'monkey chatter' to a background level, and then to not notice anymore.

This is achieving the first fundamental step of mind focus. Habit replacement takes a great part in this process as we shift our thinking habits, good thinking becomes the norm, rather than being prey to 'the monkey'.

Now do:

Reflection - Don't forget to write down your own thoughts and experiences on these exercises for assessment.

Meditation is as simple as a thought. Do not make the mistake of looking for complexity in simplicity.

Meditation is as unique as it is common. The very fact it blends these dualities and makes them one is its power. This is the first stage of unifying your mind and body through the energy arts.

Mind focus.

Stillness is standing with calm in a storm. Observant, and in control

Meditation

Course 2 - Intermediate

Principles to consider:

- Visualisation.

- Being mindful with and beyond breath

Exercise 1: Practicing directing your thoughts whilst breathing.

Exercise 2: Reflection - Don't forget to write down your own thoughts and experiences on these exercises for assessment.

Exercise: **Visualisations**

The mind is powerful and will go where you want it to go if you have the will and control to make it go there, now we have avoided the monkey chatter we can further discipline ourselves to hold a thought focus and make a visualisation, similar to those used in hypnotisms, purely as a relaxing stimulus.

Let us do the 'transport meditation' which places us in another place, a beach, or a forest, or a cool quiet cave by the sea.

This is simple, we attain our comfortable position, begin our focus on our breathing, this time we imagine our breath filling us up to the extremity of our limbs, all the way to our hands and feet and as we feel that feeling of focus arriving we can count to ten and upon gaining ten we see ourselves arriving in our chosen place of beauty and calm. It is often good to put ourselves in places of nature, as this has resonant benefits which will be explained in further courses.

So we feel the hot sand under our feet on the beach, the cool breeze blowing in off the sea, and the gulls crying in the sky, it is all comfortable and there is nothing around to stress you.

Your walk is equally comfortable, no illnesses or injuries bother you on this walk, and you can even run if you wish and enjoy the water. Sometimes the mind, like when the monkey chatters will throw up something bad on the beach, the test here is the same as before, we go back to our focus of the hot sand, the beach, the cool breeze, the feelings of comfort, and we carry on. If whatever bad persists, we go back to focus purely on the breathing.

This is all natural, and is the path we must walk to gain focus. This bad is your minds neuroses of anxiety and doubts. As you practice this walk on the beach, it will get easier and easier to maintain the focus and these doubts will recede. It is simply practice.

We take a similar step to exit the meditation by counting down from 10 to 1, we awake a little more on each step until we reach 1 and then we can become aware, slowly of our environment again, begin to move and stretch a little but don't get up yet. Just rest for a while and allow your body to wake itself up naturally. You may feel a bit spaced out but you will feel very relaxed and refreshed.

Once we can create this meditation environment for ourselves more easily we can use this 'beach' as a venue for further exercises to strengthen the mind focus.

Another visualisation this time twinned with breathing meditation we can perform is the smoke/light meditation:

This consists of the same comfortable posture you've found for yourself from before and on the breath in, visualise breathing in light, on the breath out, breathing out smoke. The light being freshness and healing and peace and positivity, the smoke meaning negativity, stagnancy, discord, stress, etc. Our minds are very powerful and this can be a way to achieve better health, if we assign values to the very air we breathe just using our imaginations. There are many variations upon this.

Reflection - Don't forget to write down your own thoughts and experiences on these exercises for assessment.

Meditation is as simple as a thought. Do not make the mistake of looking for complexity in simplicity.

Meditation is as unique as it is common. The very fact it blends these dualities and makes them one is its power. This is the first stage of unifying your mind and body through the energy arts.

Mind focus.

Stillness is standing with calm in a storm. Observant, and in control.

Meditation

Course 3 - Advanced

Principles to consider

- Repetition

Repetition - Do a common household chore with the theme of repetition in your mind, make this task a mantra - a repetition that becomes automatic and soothing.

Repetition is soothing and is a good way to bridge the gap between only being able to meditate in posture or at home in a quiet space and taking it towards to the next level of being able to switch on the meditational state when you need it to calm yourself or achieve focus for a task at hand.

The best tasks to begin this with are ones that people describe as 'therapeutic', that are repetitious by nature.

Folding clothes for example, or vacuuming, or any number of household chores are repetitive.

Focus on the repetition, and it will become soothing.

Once your mind has got past the irritation stage of ' I could be doing more interesting things ' after a time you will notice that the repetition begins to refocus the mind and give it something to occupy itself with and the irritation aspect will vanish. Eventually the irritation could well switch to the task ending!

The most basic and universal form of this is walking.

How many times if we get upset or stressed do we go for a walk?

It settles the mind partially due to the rhythm of the feet, the monotony and rhythm.

Exercise: **Meditational Walking**

Pick a route you know well, this again is beneficial for meditation as this will also be repetitious for the mind to see a familiar context.

Then...

Go for a walk. This is a very valuable exercise for awareness and will set you up nicely to learn about energy in the next course.

Whilst you are walking become very aware of breathing, and your footsteps, become aware of the kind of mental space this puts you in, and try and make a mental imprint of that feeling/mind state. When movement AND breathing AND mind focus become one in the mind, this can be very powerful. When you get home, note down the difference from when you went out, use a simple scale of 1-10. How you felt before you left, and how you felt when you got back, in terms of how much energy you feel you have, and how relaxed you feel.

Reflection - Don't forget to write down your own thoughts and experiences on these exercises for assessment.

Meditation is as simple as a thought. Do not make the mistake of looking for complexity in simplicity.

Meditation is as unique as it is common. The very fact it blends these dualities and makes them one is its power. This is the first stage of unifying your mind and body through the energy arts.

Mind focus.

Stillness is standing with calm in a storm. Observant, and in control.

The Author breaking a freestanding board

The Energy Arts Course 2: Energy

Some notes on human Energy:

Recognition, awareness of and moving it with the mind-

A short treatise on energies that humans produce:

As a Westerner myself, I have found that the best way to both convince other westerners of the existence of and explain Chi/Qi/Ki is using a few analogies.

One is 'Bioenergy'; this is the best as it covers all the others.

Another is body electricity - what we have running our brain, nervous system and consequently everything else, we don't know where it starts, this 'life spark' but like Frankenstein we know it's the beginning. It just IS and it's the source of life. We can therefore say that because every living being runs on similar energies there is a planetary network and therefore a universal one because there must be a source. Divine energy.

As discussed later, Yin and Yang requires both heaven and earth. (Projection and reception) so it cannot be just Earthbound in nature.

Another analogy is what they say in China, that Chi lives in the blood.

In my own mind, I think there is a chi 'trinity' composed of the three elements in our reality which are always in flux.

That is electricity, fire, and water.

Personally I think chi lives in a combination of these. In training in Chinese martial and healing arts I have come across fire chi training and water chi training, in training in Japanese healing and martial arts I have come across Reiki healing which often feels hot, or cold and can cause a small electrical shocking sensation, which requires no physical contact from the healer. Often in use chi also feels like a rippling or pouring through the body, like water. Water is also used to describe the human mind:

"Empty your mind, be formless. Shapeless, like water. If you put water into a cup, it becomes the cup. You put water into a bottle and it becomes the bottle. You put it in a teapot it becomes the teapot. Now, water can flow or it can crash. Be water my friend."

-Bruce Lee

This is an interesting quote as Lee points out the Yin Yang nature of a Yin element, that it can crash (Yang) or flow (Yin), he bestows upon the water a human will.

35

Water is the premiere adaptive substance in nature. Water flows and so does chi. Water is the philosophic understanding of chi

I feel that electricity and fire and water best describe its manifest human experience.

Water - philosophic/physical gateway.

Electricity - Yin. Fire - yang.

It is POLAR in nature.

Negative/receiving (Yin) -

Positive/projecting (Yang) -

Both these are generated by our bodies through the major element that we are made up from. WATER. You could say that we make a choice and water translates it. YIN YANG represents the CHOICE.

So our INTENT moves through the WATER and results in Yin or Yang action. Yin or Yang is not decided consciously, it is decided by what we do. Our bodies code these energies automatically. The best way we can understand and recognise the YIN YANG energies is by experiencing them through set pieces (actions or meditations)

Seeking an example in popular culture, in the Matrix film Morpheus speaks of the matrix as being everywhere you

36

look, energy is the same. Energy IS the world it's only our interacting with it that we translate as solid reality. Some world philosophies therefore state reality is an illusion. To all intents and purposes it isn't an illusion, it's a resonant vibration and that is still actual.

Humans ARE batteries in terms of Yin and Yang, and Neo is healed using acupuncture style techniques when he is first disconnected from 'The Matrix'.

As far as practicality goes, we can delve into duality too deeply, and get confused. For instance, Generally Earth is described as YIN, yet Old Chinese texts on the subject describe:

"According to the earliest comprehensive dictionary of Chinese characters (ca. 100 CE), Xu Shen's Shuowen jiezi *(Explaining Single-component Graphs and Analyzing Compound Characters),* yin *refers to "a closed door, darkness and the south bank of a river and the north side of a mountain."* Yang *refers to "height, brightness and the south side of a mountain.""*

From http://www.iep.utm.edu/yinyang/

From this we can see how complex it can get the further we go into detail and split concepts into aspects. This book is about USE not just THEORY. Put another way categorisation is not always your friend. It becomes obsessive and the emphasis then becomes purely cerebral and results in a disconnect. Emotional intelligence and felt truth is what is needed rather than just a stream of absolute facts.

Again, OUR BODY ALREADY KNOWS AND PRODUCES THESE ENERGIES AUTOMATICALLY TO MATCH OUR ACTIONS.

Returning to the concept of Divine energy we can travel to Japan to explore the 5 rings:

Earth, water, fire, wind, sky

Many male/female attributes are given here, wind is likened to the human mind and sky is an additional concept meaning void, heaven, or essentially spirit, anything not of this world. Traditionally martial artists have used this frame to connect with the quintessence, a concept that could be termed the collective unconscious. This concept also has a parallel in India: **Śūnyatā.**

The Chakras

The Chakra system is an ambient eventuality emanating from the electro chemical processes of our body. The human body generates a lot of electricity and where the concentrations of it are densest; there are the chakras, invisible wheels of rotating energy, floating just above our skin.

The Meridians

The Meridians are energy pathways that follow the major nerve centres of the body, they form a 'matrix' and an electrical modulation system for our unconscious body functions. In energy terms, they keep us ticking along nicely and keep the energy flowing.

People with an understanding of and great levels of chi are charismatic and magnetic with great physical endurance to toxins and stresses.

Becoming attuned or consciously aware of your own Chi also attunes you to other peoples and so your basic awareness expands to include other people's energy. People who have trained in the energy arts can influence your own energy quite powerfully through just being around them, your own energy can be 'patterned' through theirs.

This can of course work both ways, very negative people can also impact your energy in a negative way and stop it moving, but we shouldn't just dump those people, as those are the ones WE are uplifting, and staying around them builds up our own strength of what is essentially character in dealing with them.

Even clairvoyance and prophecy can be attributed to this concept of becoming aware and connecting to the divine energy pervading all creation. Of course if God is eternal there is no reason why chi should also not be timeless so precognition could be possible.

Also connecting with (thought/ intention/ feeling) to another individual who is 'plugged in' could well be possible. After all, recognition of another individual is not just facial or physical, while a 'sixth sense' may be faint; it is always there and often called by the layman a 'funny feeling'.

Chi can be used to delay or speed up. To delay damage to the body or speed up healing, to slow down time in combat or to accelerate your own speed and power. These will be explored further in the last part of the energy arts - Meditation and energy.

Now that we have done meditation we can begin to find out that energy follows intent. Where our minds attention goes, our energy goes with it.

A word on energy healing.

Energy healing is all about intent, just as causing any energy movement is all about intent.

Acupuncture, already briefly mentioned, works by conducting the meridians or energy pathways and redirecting chi one way or another.

This is not a book about acupuncture which is a very exact science that is happily gaining popularity in the west.

Reiki is another form of energy therapy, which claims to channel ambient energy through the healer; in this respect it is identical to faith healing.

A simple way of healing yourself is, again with your intent, with your mind, and the same strength that can be used to shatter bricks and boards can be used and directed to heal. All energy is the same and we change it with our intent.

Energy

Course 1

Beginner

Concepts:

- Externalizing

- Energy in environment

Main principles:

- Mind direction

- Energy resonation

- Connecting with the natural world to

- Rebalance and reenergize after being in an artificial environment.

There are easy ways to produce and rejuvenate energy. One of these is to rebalance your own by resonating with the natural world. Trees, plants, nature. We are after all a part of creation, and the energy patterns of creation also run through us, it is an energetic osmosis.

One of the best ways to experience this is to walk barefoot upon the earth, to connect physically with plants and trees and other living organisms.

In urban society we have less greenery, we have concrete, plastics, artificial materials that have no life force of their own, and plenty of MAN MADE resonance like TV and radio transmissions, WIFI, manmade electricity.

These all have an effect on our natural resonance, and though they may not be immediately harmful as such, they are definitely oppressive, and sometimes overly stimulating of the natural bio-energies (electricity of the nervous system/chi) of the body.

Therefore we can become misaligned energy wise by living in this kind of created artificial environment.

Our immediate environment is YIN, this is why it is called Mother Nature, the Directive and moral part of our spirit is yang.

This is reflected in the natural roles of a mother and father in bringing up a child. The mother creates and maintains a healthy material environment; the father tends to make directive decisions for the child's path and behaviours.

These are tendencies and rely more on how pre-dominant energies behave rather than personalities.

Exercise: **Natural Energy Meditation**

Sit on grass, in a garden, or in a park. Feet and hands bare, both palms and soles of the feet flat to the floor. See pic for suggested posture.

Feel the earth beneath you, visualise it as a current of energy just like the electricity than runs your own nervous system. Visualise sucking that energy up into yourself, through your hands and feet, soothing and taking away the harsh manmade energies you have absorbed which impregnate our environment. Think of re - resonating, of bringing your frequency back into matching that of the earth and trees, plants, sky, weather, rocks etc.

You can also do this meditation with a manmade source of resonation, a computer, a laptop, a TV, with one hand, just to feel the harsh resonant frequencies, and then you will be better to feel the smooth natural ones in nature. It is an exercise of feeling/reaching out with your mind into an object or the environment.

Just walking barefoot upon the earth is a free foot massage as well and good for your feet and posture.

This meditation concentrates on resonating with the energy of the earth beneath us and of the nature around us and so this is where our mind should be, it is meant to cleanse us of artificial manmade energies by resonating with nature rather than a manmade environment.

We can do this by meditating (mind focusing) on the feel of the earth through these two very sensitive areas of our body. In classical energy systems the palms and soles of the feet contain energy centres which are secondary chakras. In this way they connect most profoundly with our environment and we can resonate with the energy of the earth through them.

The elements as ideas can also be meditated upon, observing water can help us resonate with the water which makes up 70% of our own bodies, for instance, to better feel our own makeup, and our own possibilities, of adaptation in movement and clarity of mind, fire, an element of internal transformation, air - breath, earth, solidity and physical presence, sky - spirituality, the world of values and ideals, prayer.

Reflection - Don't forget to write down your own thoughts and experiences on these exercises for assessment.

Energy appears in USE, it is not just a series of thoughts.

Heaven Meditation

Energy

Course 2

Intermediate

Concepts:

Heaven and Earth Meditation

Main Principles:

- The Diaphragm principle.

- Movement twinned with breath.

Exercise: Heaven and Earth meditation

This is an energy balancing chi gung meditation exercise in two parts based upon the diaphragm principle. That is expansion and compression. It is meant to balance the three main energy axis of the body. The central, from the crown to the perineum, and left and right from the top of the shoulder down through the hip and the leg to the sole of the foot.

It is done on the right and left side to balance the left and right sides of the body energetically as well as the heaven and earth vertically. The diaphragm principle here makes use of the knees and elbows.

In the first part of the exercise: Stand normally with knees slightly bent if possible, shoulder width apart. Breathe in through your nose , placing your tongue against the top of your mouth throughout the duration of the exercise, (the front and back of the human body are like two poles of a battery, doing this is like completing a circuit) as you breathe in bend your knees and allow your hands to rise as in Fig 1.

 Breathing out, again through the nose, straighten your knees and push your palms up towards the heavens, rotating them inward as you do so, to achieve the maximum distribution of energy. (Fig 2)

Repeat this a minimum of 3 times, do it ponderously - and be mindful of how you feel. Without a pause, which you will be able to do after practice, enter the second part of the exercise - go straight from reaching for the heavens in Fig 2, breathing out, to Fig 3, breathing in, as before with bent knees and the hands close to the body, on the breath in, one by the ear and one by the waist.

The hands are straight to begin with, heels of the palms facing in. Breathing out through the nose the knees and arms straighten simultaneously and the arms twist so the heels of the palms point outward (see Fig 4).

Just as you are about to lock out your elbows and knees, start to breath in, as you do, reverse the direction of movement, your knees start to bend and your arms twist back and down towards your body to return to heel of palms inwards.

Again, repeat, then switch sides (Fig 5-6).

Reflection - Don't forget to write down your own thoughts and experiences on these exercises for assessment.

Fig 1

Fig 2

Fig 3

Fig 4

Fig 5

Fig 6

Energy appears in USE, it is not just a series of thoughts.

Energy

Course 3

Advanced

Main Principles:

- Yin /Yang (Duality)

- A focused useful Moving meditation with energy

- Incorporating course 1 and 2 together.

- Incidental breathing.

- (Breath follows movement)

This exercise is based on aspects of tai chi as well as chi gung.

The main difference to this exercise is the breathing follows the movement; just let your body decide when to breathe. It will know.

The joints of the body are very important when allowing energy to flow or immediately changing character of that energy. Looking at the two postures in this simple exercise we can see that one is open and welcoming whilst the other is closed and defensive and slightly threatening.

Energy flows better through open joints. In the Yin picture all the joints are open allowing the movement to decide and motivate the energy flow, whilst in the Yang picture the energy is being 'stored' and 'built up' and quite possibly in health terms trapped.

In Yin yang terms the front of the body is Yin and the back of the body is Yang. Yin is the soles of the feet and the palms of the hands, and the face, genitals and throat. We all can see that that our inner forearms and thighs are more sensitive than the outside, as well as for the sole and top of the feet.

Yin (receiving/open) posture

Yang (closed/projecting) posture

Exercise: **Experiencing Yin/Yang energy**

This exercise is not complicated. Simple start in the YIN posture in the photo, move forward into a normal standing position and step forward into the YIN posture on the opposite side (right foot/hand forward)

Then step forward again into a standing position. Settle a moment then step forward into the Yang position with your right side, step forward again to a standing position, and then step forward into the Yang position with your left foot/hand forward.

Again, the breathing should follow the movement, the mind should be present and alert to the changes of energy you feel, from vulnerability and openness to an aggressive closedness. Yang incidentally doesn't have to be ANGRY it is just positive, directive, dry, and aggressive.

A good example comes from the martial arts. An open handed strike extends energy, whilst a fist begins to **'hold onto'** it.

Yin	Yang
Open	Closed
Receiving	Projecting
Soft	Hard
Female	Male
Dark	Light
Passive	Aggressive
Environmental	Directive

When performing this exercise, you can utilise the table of yin and yang values. Pick say 'soft' and when you are performing the Yin posture, meditate upon the meaning of this word and feel softness in yourself.

Likewise, you may pick 'aggressive' and meditate upon that in the Yang part of the exercise.

You may also pick an opposite value and do the YIN exercise meditating upon hardness.

Doing this you will begin to develop an idea of this concept.

It is NOT necessary to only project YANG or YIN consciously as your body will do this correspondingly; however it will help you top further feel the energies.

This is an **IDENTIFICATION** exercise only. A mind exercise.

In actuality Yin is in Yang and Yang is in Yin and this is healthy, it is not healthy to unbalance yourself.

Reflection - Don't forget to write down your own thoughts and experiences on these exercises for assessment.

Energy appears in USE, it is not just a series of thoughts.

The Energy Arts Course 3:
Meditation And Energy

Meditation develops the mind focus for you to be able to direct your bioenergy.

- Thought

- Use

- Intent

(Imagination. Intent. Feeling.)

Simply:

1. Meditation - isolate the thought.

2. Energy - feel and get to know your energy; recognise the 'flavour' of it.

3. Meditation AND energy use your thoughts to push your energy around your body and to concentrate it and project it externally.

Energy transforms from yin to yang and back again in our bodies according to SOMETHING WE ARE DOING AT THE TIME. It is an AUTOMATIC PROCESS. So by practicing certain tasks we can increase our energy flow.

Nebulous substances electricity fire and air energy in flux. (Plasma, 4th state of matter), these are similar states to mind.

Without imagination you cannot control your Chi. Imagination is the same as visualisation. Without it you cannot extend your mind. Also:

Do not believe that facts are more important than truth.

Truth is the way forward, whilst facts are past and established. They can only be added to.

Imagination is not just 'stories'. It is the force in which we can use our chi and reach forward in our personal lives to discover our context in the wider scheme of things. Especially in relation to others. It is a key.

Once imagination is used enough with intent and through performing a set piece it starts to become automatic.

The Author teaching in the Great Outdoors

Extending awareness into a Weapon

Energy and Meditation

Course 1

Beginner

Concepts:

- Finding/ feeling your own bioenergy part 1

Exercise: Finding and Feeling Bioenergy

Pinch your arm, note the pain, note the feeling use your mind to control the pain and disconnect that part of your body from the rest. This is called discompartmentalisation and can be done instantly using imagination which directs your chi.

Pinch your leg note how your attention goes to that point on your body. without pinching your leg, be aware of that exact same part of the body you just pinched, put all your attention there, feel what the skin is feeling, what the flesh is feeling, now move your attention up your leg, down your leg, fast, slow, will part of the leg to become warmer, colder. Pick a small spot to begin with.

Reflection - Don't forget to write down your own thoughts and experiences on these exercises for assessment.

Exercise: Finding and Feeling Bioenergy Pt2

Concepts:

- Finding/ feeling your own bioenergy part 2

Twitch your pectoral muscle.

Find a muscle you don't normally use.

Try and control the tensing of the muscle, if you can already do the pectoral muscle find another.

Note the feeling before you can achieve it. It is building new neuron pathways in the brain, like learning a new technique in martial arts. Learning to control your chi is also an unfamiliar feeling, its results are not tension but 'fizziness', heat, cold 'sparkiness ' and vibration.

Reflection - Don't forget to write down your own thoughts and experiences on these exercises for assessment.

The body is all about the mind. The mind is all about energy.

Energy and Meditation

Course 2

Intermediate

Concepts:

- Unifying mind and body

Exercise: Unifying Mind and Body

Get a pencil. Put it on a table. Sit at the table. Pick up the pencil in your right hand, put it down again. Note the feeling.

Now ONLY IN YOUR MIND, using YOUR IMAGINATION, pick up the pencil again, feeling the action you just performed, without actually physically doing it. Repeat the above two steps. Now do them at the same time.

- Reflection - Don't forget to write down your own thoughts and experiences on these exercises for assessment.

-

The body is all about the mind. The mind is all about energy.

Course 3:

Advanced

Exercise: Moving from the Centre

The centre of our body is just below the navel, and that is the most powerful place to move from.

Practice the start of every movement starting from the hips, even moving your arm. You can start any bodily movement from the centre of the body, what the Chinese call the lower Dantien, another term for energy centre, like the term chakra. A very easy way of doing this is to relax your arms totally and turn your waist back and forth, your arms will follow suit without you doing anything.

Reflection - Don't forget to write down your own thoughts and experiences on these exercises for assessment

The body is all about the mind. The mind is all about energy.

Final Exercise

Now we unify all aspects in one practice.

Before we have done - Meditation.

Comprising:

    1.   Isolating and focusing thought

    2.   Visualisation

    3.   Repetition/mantra/trance.

We have also done - Energy

Comprising:

    1)   Motion

    2)   Awareness of self/Yin Yang/duality

    3)   Compression/expansion.

    4)   Resonation

Now we must achieve:

Unification of all the above plus:

- Intent

- Projection.

---This is simpler than it sounds

Unification Final Exercise

- All the aspects of meditation can be done whilst moving.

- We must first design a movement as a vehicle.

- Any movement can be repetitious.

Large movements produce lots of flowing energy. Open and closed postures can produce different types of energy along with tension and relaxation.

If we do this exercise in nature we create resonance.

At this stage, breathing patterns are controlled by the movement; the movement is not controlled by the timing of the breathing.

Any movements can be done with these UNIFYING factors and CONCEPTS in mind, go out and start and design your own exercise. Dictating anything other than principles at this point would breed a love of technique rather than principle and stunt your own growth.

And projection?

Feel your own energy whilst doing this self-designed exercise and when you can, try projecting it with both a gesture of your body and your mind as in exercise 3.

As discussed earlier in this book this will facilitate your connection with the energy of others and environment, this unification is the gateway to what some call a sixth sense but it is really a natural function of unifying yourself.

Reflection - Don't forget to write down your own thoughts and experiences on these exercises for assessment.

The body is all about the mind. The mind is all about energy.

Course Ends

The author performing a chi gung form

Further Reflections on Energy

This chapter is full of other ideas and thoughts and realisations about energy, this part is like a journal. This format often works very much better in assimilating information and concepts, a chunk at a time; it tends to give in my own experience a greater understanding in a philosophical/experiential way of thinking about this subject rather than purely cognitive.

A short paragraph can hold much more meaning when considered than a whole book even, and the whole history of energy teaching abounds with such literary thoughts and expressions to describe experience of the world of energy.

There may be theories which haven't been substantiated, varying perspectives on concepts already explored, and explained in various different ways, and I have included a personal testimony to **'The energy arts'.**

Time

Imagination is not bound by time.

For instance when we use martial technique to break an object, if we are trained and capable, we are WHOLLY in that moment just before contact in contact and just after with the object. Time slows down; our energy bursts through the object.

Time before: energy 'swell' - potential energy transforms to kinetic energy via intent of the mind driving the ENERGY of the nervous system to drive the body. (People always say - aim through the object - that requires imagination through visualisation)

Contact: the energy is transferred into and moves through the object to be broken.

Just after: A bursting is felt as the energy passes through the object and becomes ambient and potentially to be used again.

Note that in the above the physics is described alongside the energetic. They are one and the same western and eastern approaches. From each end of the spectrum meeting in the centre. Mind is not wholly material, thought is not wholly material.

To build up a way to use energy we must use first body then mind before we can then attain more use of just intent itself rather than just mind.

Large gestures of the body can be made smaller gestures until they are shrunk to become merely thoughts and projections of energy as a result.

The future:

Remote location.

Using Your Imagination:

Remember the way someone FEELS. Remember their energy signature. Be guided to them; be aware of when they think of you.

Meditation is just like external martial arts, it can be long frame or short frame

.....To start to meditate for long periods to find the keys, with practice, to meditate for shorter periods to get the same effect, until it becomes instant, with a thought you can enter the energy state instantly.

Yin yoga (environment), yang prayer (direction)

People will often NOT respect a system UNLESS it IS complicated, ritualised, secret in some way, and expensive. (Desirable)

Reach out into the environment with your senses, and so your intentionality and your CHI. listen outside to the cars, to the sound of your own breath, the whine of your own nervous system.

The experiments of Masaru Emoto have uncovered the possibility of the power of intentionality.

(Energy affecting the environment)

Reach out energetically with a stick and make it truly part of your body, try and feel with it rather than just strike.

Reach out and meditate with the brick, put your mind into it. If I was a mystic I would say talk to the spirit of the brick, and it will agree to break for you when you want it to.

At the most basic form

Meditation is mind focus

Energy is awareness of your own chi

Combining the two allows you to focus completely on your energy with INTENT via mind focus to achieve healing and break objects.

Improvised Chi Gung Form Based On Principles

Principles of moving chi gung

- Expansion compression
- Open close joints,
- Palms in out yin/yang.
- Mind focus
- Breathing follows movement
- Speed (build/release) relaxation/tension

Get to know sympathetic resonance of an object/person etc by spending time with them in meditative state of INSTANT MEDITATION.

Find the meditative state, remember its energy /feeling and switch to it when you need to.

Human battery perineum and dantien poles

Mind has an inherent technique for using energy; it KNOWS when yin or yang is appropriate. For breaking, it will not use YIN it will become YANG as it externalises.

Even so getting to know the 'flavour' of the energy is important then you can even better feel what energies you are producing... The Yin/Yang exercise in the meditation course is designed to facilitate this.

In martial terms the hard and soft chi are very important and relate directly to dynamic tension and relaxation respectively

----

Interaction with energy in 'flux' like fire is good to develop chi, as its nature is similar.

Energy is not magic, not secret, and not mystical. These are just barriers people use to teach BS rituals and unnecessary cultural aspects and to make money from it.

This why there's so much BS and fear surrounding this subject.

However, energy is so much a part of us, literally it's what we are, that we cannot recognise it. It's hiding under our very nose, IN our very nose in fact, so another reason why such a weight of complicated ritual and technique has been created is to create objectivity and a way for the mind to gain control over it.

This is the way I've been taught. It may not be the way you want to be taught. Tough. It is what it is.

It is long term teaching. You may feel something today you may not.

Some people don't take as long as others with it. Patience is key.

It helps to have faith in things you cannot see.

Take the view that you don't know what it is yet and don't have all the answers and you may discover it in yourself more swiftly.

Energy is a new limb.

You need to feel the new limb before you can use it.

Sometimes you will have use adrenalin. That is different. Adrenalin is anaesthetic and a muscle accelerant.

Energy is your mind intent focused through your body.

It is akin to what Bruce lee said- 'a finger pointing at the moon' sometimes in life this happens anyway, things just spontaneously line up and we act with mind as well as body. This happens more and more as we practice.

It is also effort, but it is not just physical effort. It is MIND effort.

Pouring all of yourself into every technique.
COMMITTING to it.

As science cannot yet measure, analyse and quantify consciousness so it can't identify intent of mind, only measure the results in the physical world.

Back to the start. Learning to use your fifth limb, your mind.

We have physical strength, and adrenalin as an accelerant.

Then when have felt and known our energy, we can add another consciousness level to the process.

Exercise. To feel it.

Pinch yourself. Hard. Note how your attention goes to the pain.

Where the attention of your mind goes, your bioenergy (chi) goes.

(Wood behaves more like bone, brick is more resonant)

Exercise. To move it.

Chi gung. Move that attention.

Learn to think of objects in the material world in terms of frequency of resonation and energy in terms of transforming it in movement and collision.

Not just of 'it's solid and more solid than me and it's heavy.'

Not in terms of just Newtonian physics.

Ego blocks chi When ego becomes involved fear is involved. Via apprehension and assumption.

Tension is not good for flowing energy.

'Don't react until it is appropriate.

Martial arts is about how much of yourself you can put into a moment of time so if you can put all the energy of your mind into a moment as well as from your physicality then you are a better martial artist.

At the end of the day, it will take as many processes for you as it does, for one person it might take one, it might take many, and it's a case of mindset and aptitude. They are all though SIMILAR as we are all SIMILAR

Chi gung is a state, it is not a technicality.

Relaxing exercises like behaving as a rag doll. Body must be relaxed to move energy, not to constrict it.

Train yourself to become relaxed when in combat with an opponent.

It is impossible to be trapped in the past, in the future or within yourself when you have to deal effectively with an outside opponent.

We are all part of this universe therefore we USE this universe.

Combat Meditation

Meditation always means you are less bipolar in energy state, instead of being relaxed with lassitude you are relaxed but READY. Fighting in meditation your breathing will also be controlled and relaxed.

Emotional intelligence.

Energy breaking is about putting your mind into a brick.

Emotional intelligence is required to identify the feeling of this process so as to remember it, meditate upon it and repeat it.

It is not a cognitive experience as much as a feelingly experiential one. Again, it is like learning to use a new limb. This feeling of remembering and trying to repeat has the effect in the brain of building a new neural pathway, as its feeling, the electrical process of the body is involved.

Think of 'mental resonance' as a key.

Nerves are full of energy, so if we strike them with energy, we can use the strike as the connection and hit other points elsewhere in the body by using mental resonance.

With chi we can slow things down or speed them up.

The matrix bullet time is a sensationalist example of this.

Meditation cuts out movement shock from other sources. It flattens the fight or flight response and makes adrenaline in this respect unneeded.

More haste less speed is a common saying, what it means is, speed is with the body only and haste is with the MIND. If you leave your mind behind, your body will be out of control. Be IN that moment with your mind IN that movement.

Speed is physical, haste is MINDAL. Use haste and your body will act appropriately.

In a fight situation, it is ok to gives strikes which impact on the surface of the opponent, even better to give strikes which penetrate the opponent, like a wave or a ripple. Hydro shock. This is why we break objects like bricks, and boards, to build that penetration of energy.

The body is all about the mind.

Moving energy about the body with the mind.

Moving energy about the body with the breath and the mind

Moving energy about the body with movement

Moving energy about the body with movement breath and mind

Movement based chi gung there is physical shrinking expanding breathing of the whole body.

Mind based posture is fixed.

Breath based posture is fixed.

In conclusion:

- Energy 'techniques' are endless, because everything is energy.

- Do everything with intent and you will use energy.

- It is indeed a five minute lesson that can take a lifetime.

- Boil everything down until it is functional, do not fall in love with theory and remember that whilst energy is common to all, it is also personal to everyone.

- The creator gave us life to use. The more of that life we can put into achievement, a moment, a project, a marriage, a job, the more we can achieve, don't be paralysed. Energy moves...

Now carry on.

Charles (Charlie) Alexander Fox

थे ऍएग्र्य् आर्ट्स - 'The Energy Arts'

http://www.theenergyarts.co.uk

A Personal Testimony

Many things that happen in this world can keep us from changing, from adapting, keep us from moving in any direction.

After several horrible traumas that happened at once in my life I was such a person. I was so dissipated, felt so powerless, standing in a constant storm as the rest of the world seemed to be at peace.

There is a way for us to take control. It is not by ego, it is by will, it is us using everything we have been given and using it for the good of ourselves. This is not self-love, this is loving ourselves. Not a will to power, a will for good.

It is acting by truth but acting on it. Doing it. Not merely thinking about it. It wasn't until I fully understood this action of energy given to us by our creator that I realized I could change things and didn't have to just be a passenger any longer. God waits for us to move before he helps us. So many people in this world are waiting for someone else to provide the impetus for them. They are stuck, frozen. Whatever faith you are, the answer is the same. Move, and use all of yourself to do it. Then, the Universe, God, Jesus, Buddha, Allah, The source, some equivalent of the laws of physics will help you, you have produced something and so you can MAKE something.

We are relatively powerful, but it is a good power -

Not domination over others, but domination over ourselves, we can achieve. We can change and adapt. THIS is spiritual growth. Frozen, we can do nothing.

The energy of the creation we live in cannot supersede the creator of that energy, but we have been given a certain mastery over our own energies. We should use them. After all each time we make a cup of tea, go to sleep, walk, anything, we use them. It is no more complicated than that, it's only a matter of urgency, focus and extent of need.

People see a mother lifting a car off her child by herself and say it is adrenalin that comes out of nowhere. No, it is herself putting all of herself into that moment, which compresses time and sparks her adrenal glands from her nervous energy, increasing the conductivity of her muscles, as her nervous system goes into overdrive and by virtue of that ENERGY she lifts the car. She has no other choice. The process starts with her MIND. The body simply reacts. We can just float along rudderless in a boat on life's sea, or we can control our direction.

The energy arts can be called the art of moving.

Be directive, everything else follows from this. Nothing comes of nothing, something comes of something.

It is the choice to learn that must be respected above all. That is progression, change, and adaptation.

Charlie Fox

Sheffield July 2014

The Author breaking a London house brick

Your Own Notes

The following pages are for your own notes: